Supreme Sailor

Phil Kettle
illustrated by Craig Smith

Distributed in
the United States of America
by Pacific Learning
P.O. Box 2723
Huntington Beach, CA
92647-0723
Website:
www.pacificlearning.com

Published by Black Hills
(an imprint of Toocool Rules
Pty Ltd)
PO Box 2073
Fitzroy MDC VIC 3065
Australia
61+3+9419-9406

First published in the United States by Black Hills in 2004.
American editorial by Pacific Learning in 2004.
Text copyright © Phillip Kettle, 2002.
Illustration copyright © Toocool Rules Pty Limited, 2002.

 a black dog and Springhill book

Printed in China through Colorcraft Ltd, Hong Kong

ISBN 1 920924 09 4
PL-6210

10 9 8 7 6 5 4 3 2 1   08 07 06 05 04

Contents

Bert

Dog

Toocool

Chapter 1
Back on Deck

I was glad to see the sun come up. It had been a long night. I wanted to get back on the yacht. I was in the middle of an important race.

I was captain of *The Boomerang*—the greatest yacht that had ever raced.

I built it myself. It only took a couple of hours.

I used a mop for the mast. Then I made an amazing sail from an old sheet that was hanging on the clothesline.

Most of the yachts in the race had a crew of ten or more sailors. All I had were Dog and Bert the Rooster.

3

Dog stood on the pointy end of the boat. I think you call it the bow—or maybe it is the bridge. Whatever it's called, it is the part that crosses the finish line first.

Bert sat under the seat. He is not a good sailor. He's a land bird, not a seabird.

Bert was the boat's alarm clock. It was his job to make sure that I got up at dawn every morning.

There is no time for sleeping late during a yacht race.

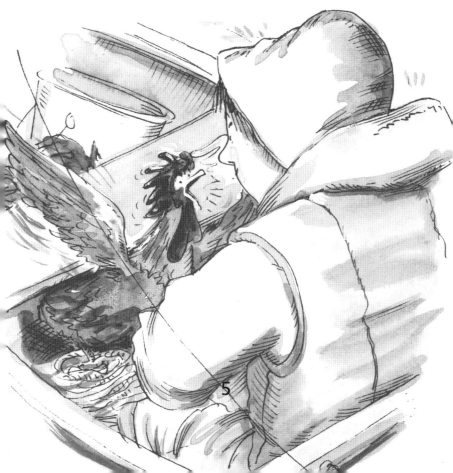

Chapter 2

Wild Ocean

Just after sunrise, the sky filled with black clouds. The waves were getting bigger.

I knew a storm was coming.

I had to keep a close eye on the weather—and on all the other yachts.

I was still in the lead, but time was running out. If another boat passed me now, it would be impossible to catch up. The conditions were far too fierce.

The yacht was rocking from side to side. The deck was creaking.

Bert the Rooster stayed down under the seat and would not come out.

He had his head tucked under his wing. I think he was feeling seasick.

The waves pounded us from every side. The boat tipped over so far that the mast almost touched the water.

These were the roughest conditions by far in this race. Other crews would be giving up and going home... but not me.

There are not many sailors as skilled or as brave as I am.

The ocean spray was soaking my face. It was getting harder for me to see, but I was tough. I could cope.

I checked my compass. We were supposed to be heading south. We were heading west!

The fierce winds had blown us off course.

Chapter 3
Dog Overboard!

I fought to steer *The Boomerang* back on course. Dog barked at the waves as they splashed over the sides.

Dog was so excited, he got too close to the edge.

A sudden wave washed him overboard.

Dog is not a good swimmer.
All he can do is dog paddle.
He was in great danger!
    I was captain of this craft.
It was my job to protect
my crew.

Without fear, I leaped into
the wild sea. Huge waves
washed over me. I sank to the
bottom.

Dog was above me, fighting
for his life. I pushed off the
bottom and swam toward him.

13

I grabbed Dog by the collar and started to swim for the yacht. It was a battle. Dog did not understand that I have taken lifesaving classes. He fought me all the way.

We fell into the boat. We were exhausted, but there was no time to waste. I had to keep working. The giant waves could drown us all at any moment.

Chapter 4
Land in the
Mist

We were now sailing at top speed, and we were going in the right direction. The finish line was not far off.

Dog was not as brave now. He sat right in the middle of the yacht.

Bert was still under the seat.

I thought he might be happier in the crow's nest. *The Boomerang* was the only yacht that had a crow's nest.

Unfortunately, no matter how hard I tried, I could not get Bert to go anywhere near the crow's nest.

Bert the Rooster has no sense of adventure.

I looked up at the sail. It
was a beautiful sail—very
colorful. It was full of wind.
It gave *The Boomerang*
great speed.

What a beautiful yacht. It
would look magnificent on the
sports channel.

The huge waves kept pounding the front of the yacht. It was hard to see through the mist. I shaded my eyes with my hands. It was no use.

I grabbed my binoculars. Yes! I could definitely see land up ahead.

I looked behind me—there was not another yacht in sight. *The Boomerang* was racing toward the finish line. We'd left all the other boats far behind.

Then I knew I was going to win the race.

I looked at my new waterproof watch. I was going to break the world record!

People everywhere would be talking about Toocool, the greatest sailor in the world.

I peered through the mist. I could not believe the size of the crowd. It was huge! They had all come to see me.

I pulled the sail down as the boat cruised into the dock.

The crowd threw flowers at me and *The Boomerang*. I waved to the crowd. It made them feel good.

I was their hero.

Chapter 5
The Crew Goes Crazy

It was time to throw the crew overboard. I think this is the custom after all victorious yacht races.

I threw Dog in first.

Then, I grabbed Bert and threw him in.

24

Bert did not seem to like the water. He jumped on Dog's back. Bert dug his claws in a little too far. Dog yelped and leaped out of the water.

The last I saw of my crew, they were running around the lemon tree barking and crowing. They did not know how to act like professionals.

I stood quietly on the deck. It was a proud moment. What a race! What a sailor!

The crowd thought I was fantastic. There was so much cheering that Mom came out to join in.

"Toocool! What are you doing with our dinghy? Just look at what you've done to my beautiful new sheet!"

Did Mom really want me to answer?

"Toocool, why can't you be like other kids?"

I just smiled to myself.

I am like other kids. The only difference is, I am also a living legend.

I am Toocool!

The End!

Toocool's
Sailing Glossary

Compass—An instrument with a needle that always points north. You use a compass to make sure you are going the right way.

Crow's nest—A box at the top of the mast. When a boat is a long way out to sea, a sailor might climb up the mast to the crow's nest to look for land.

Dock—A platform in the water where boats can be tied up when they are not being used.

Mast—A tall pole that holds up the sail on a yacht.

29

The Far Horizon

Yonder Chicken Coop
(and Bleachers)

The Faucet

The Wild Wet

Toocool

Toocool's Quick Summary
Sailing

Sailboats can be many different shapes and sizes. Some boats are so small they only need one person to sail them. Then there are the big yachts that race on the ocean. These boats have many crew members.

All sailboats need wind to move. When the wind blows, it fills the sails with air and pushes the boat through the water. The harder the wind blows, the faster the boat goes.

When you sail in the same direction the wind is blowing, it's called sailing before the wind. Sometimes the wind isn't blowing the way you want to go. When this happens, you have to zigzag across the water. This is called tacking.

Before you set sail, you should make sure you are totally prepared. I am a great sailor, but I still obey these two rules: always wear a life jacket, and always tell someone where you are going. Then you will be ready to sail. As they say on the high seas, "Anchors aweigh."

The *Boomerang*

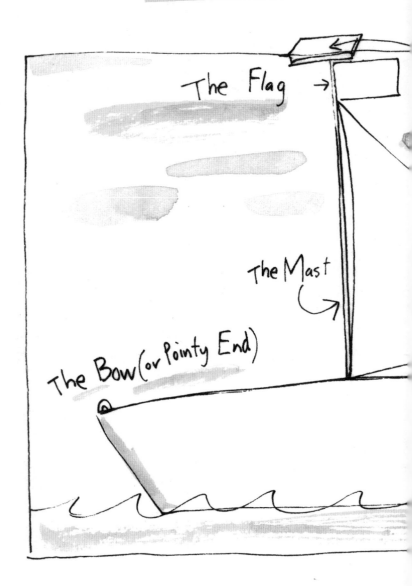

The Flag →

The Mast

The Bow (or Pointy End)

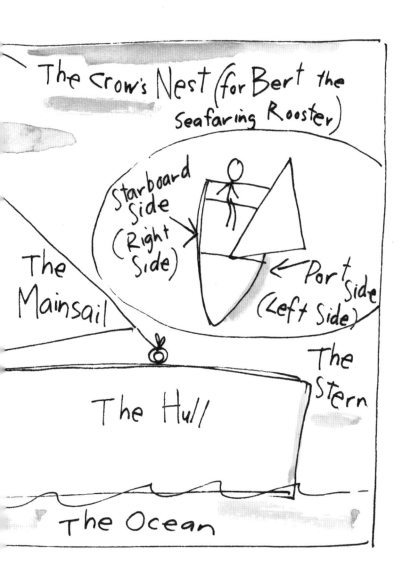

The Crow's Nest (for Bert the Seafaring Rooster)

Starboard Side (Right Side)

Port Side (Left Side)

The Mainsail

The Stern

The Hull

The Ocean

Q & A with Toocool
He Answers His Own Questions

What makes a good sailor?
A good sailor like me has lots of skills. I know how to tie knots. I am also very strong, so I can hoist the sail by myself.

Have you ever been seasick?
No. I have great sea legs. That means I don't get sick when I am on a boat.

What is your most important sailing safety tip?

Wear a life jacket. You should always wear a life jacket—even if you are a supreme sailor and an excellent swimmer, like me.

What are your favorite kinds of sailboats?

I like sailboats that stay afloat. It's not much fun to sail in a leaky boat. I am really good at sailing all kinds of boats. My favorite boats are the big yachts that are used for ocean racing. Big yachts have lots of crew members, and I can be the captain and yell out the orders. "Scrub those decks! Climb the mast! Change the sails! Bring me some chocolate milk!"

What are *port* and *starboard*? They are tricky sailing words. I know everything about sailing, so I know what they mean. Imagine you are on a boat facing the front. Port is the left-hand side of the boat, and starboard is the right-hand side.

Will you enter the round-the-world-by-yourself sailing race? I would have to think about that. I know that I would win the race, but it takes a long time to sail around the world. I might get a little bit lonely without Dog around. Who would I talk to? I think I will stick to smaller races for a while.

Who is the best all-time sailor?

The explorers who sailed around the world were pretty good sailors. They had huge crews to help them, though. I win races with just Dog and Bert the Rooster as my crew. That takes talent. That's what makes me a supreme sailor!

Sailing Quiz
How Much Do You Know about Sailing?

Q1 Where is the best place to go sailing?
A. On the ocean. *B.* In the backyard. *C.* In the bathtub.

Q2 What do you call the pointy end of a boat?
A. Bow. *B.* Stern. *C.* Spike.

Q3 What does a navigator do?
A. Cook the meals. *B.* Plan the trip. *C.* Scrub the decks.

Q4 What would you do if you were asked to drop the anchor? *A.* Hope it didn't land on your foot. *B.* Take the rope off the anchor and throw the anchor overboard. *C.* Throw the anchor overboard with the rope attached.

Q5 What is tacking? *A.* Something you use when you go fishing. *B.* Sailing on a zigzag course. *C.* Sailing the same way as the wind is blowing.

Q6 What would you do if a crew member fell overboard? *A.* Wave good-bye to them. *B.* Throw them a rope. *C.* Jump in after them.

Q7 What does a rudder do?

A. Makes the boat go where you want to. *B.* Catches fish.

C. Cleans the bottom of the boat.

Q8 What makes the boat go faster?

A. The mast. *B.* The crow's nest.

C. The wind.

Q9 Should you wear a life jacket when sailing?

A. Only if you can't swim.

B. Always. *C.* Only if you can't see land from the boat.

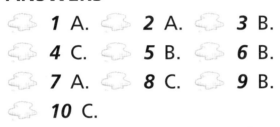

Q10 What would you do if you wanted sailing lessons? **A.** Ask a lifeguard. **B.** Practice with a toy boat in the bathtub. **C.** Ask Toocool.

ANSWERS

1 A.   **2** A.   **3** B.

4 C.   **5** B.   **6** B.

7 A.   **8** C.   **9** B.

10 C.

If you got ten questions right, you have sea legs. If you got more than five right, you can sit in the crow's nest. If you got fewer than five right, stay in the bathtub.

TOOCOOL

Gocart Genius

Every kid on the block has signed up for the great Gocart Race, but there can only be one winner.

Titles in the Toocool series